Helping the Environment
Pollinator Gardens

by Nick Rebman

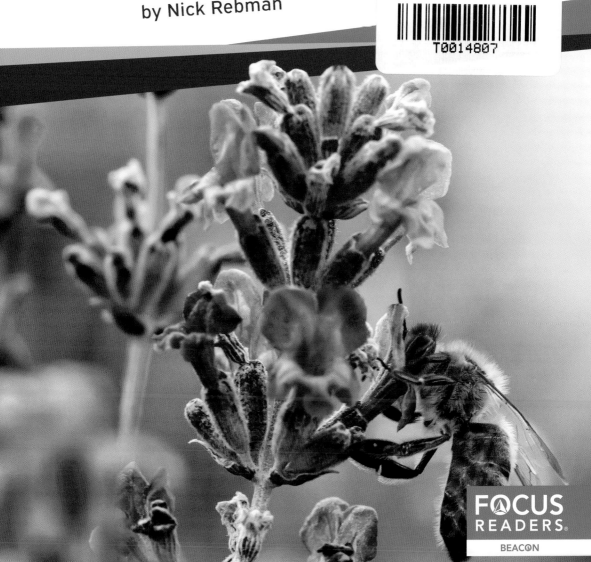

T0014807

FOCUS READERS.

READERS.

BEACON

www.focusreaders.com

Copyright © 2022 by Focus Readers®, Lake Elmo, MN 55042. All rights reserved. No part of this book may be reproduced or utilized in any form or by any means without written permission from the publisher.

Focus Readers is distributed by North Star Editions:
sales@northstareditions.com | 888-417-0195

Produced for Focus Readers by Red Line Editorial.

Photographs ©: Shutterstock Images, cover, 1, 4, 7, 11, 14, 17; iStockphoto, 8, 22, 25, 29; Patrick Kobernus/USFWS, 13; David Peterson/USFWS, 18; Frances M. Roberts/Newscom/USFWS, 20–21; Sam Stukel/USFWS, 27

Library of Congress Cataloging-in-Publication Data
Names: Rebman, Nick, author.
Title: Pollinator gardens / by Nick Rebman.
Description: Lake Elmo, MN : Focus Readers, [2022] | Series: Helping the environment | Includes index. | Audience: Grades 2-3
Identifiers: LCCN 2021011156 (print) | LCCN 2021011157 (ebook) | ISBN 9781644938386 (hardcover) | ISBN 9781644938843 (paperback) | ISBN 9781644939307 (ebook) | ISBN 9781644939734 (pdf)
Subjects: LCSH: Pollinators--Juvenile literature. | Pollination--Juvenile literature. | Plant-pollinator relationships--Juvenile literature.
Classification: LCC QK926 .R43 2022 (print) | LCC QK926 (ebook) | DDC 571.8/642--dc23
LC record available at https://lccn.loc.gov/2021011156
LC ebook record available at https://lccn.loc.gov/2021011157

Printed in the United States of America
Mankato, MN
082021

About the Author

Nick Rebman enjoys reading, drawing, and taking long walks with his dog. He lives in Minnesota.

Table of Contents

Chapter 1

A Busy Garden

The garden buzzes with activity. A bee flies from one flower to another. Soon, a butterfly lands on a purple flower. It takes a sip of nectar. This sweet liquid gives the butterfly energy.

Bees and butterflies feed on flowers. They also help plants grow.

Later, a hummingbird sticks its long beak into a red flower. It drinks nectar, too. The bird seems to float in place. Its wings move so quickly that they are a blur.

A girl and her grandfather watch the birds and insects. They love spending time in their garden.

Did You Know?

Dead leaves and branches can be helpful in gardens. Many insects make their homes in them.

 Planting flowers for pollinators can be an easy way to experience nature.

It is beautiful. It is also helping our planet. The garden is a place where pollinators can eat and live.

Chapter 2

Pollinator Problems

Pollen is a powder. It comes from the flowers of plants. Some animals help spread pollen. These animals are known as pollinators. When pollen spreads, new plants can grow.

 Pollen sticks to a bee's body. Some of the pollen falls off when the bee lands on another flower.

Most pollinators are insects. They include bees, butterflies, and beetles. Some birds are pollinators. Many bats are pollinators, too.

However, pollinators are facing threats. One problem is **habitat** loss. In many areas, people are clearing away **native** plants. When this happens, pollinators lose their homes. They also lose their food.

Pesticides are another threat. Farmers spray these chemicals on their crops. The pesticides kill the

Many people have lawns instead of growing native plants. That leads to habitat loss for pollinators.

animals and plants that harm crops.

But the chemicals often harm

pollinators, too.

   Climate change is also a threat.

The temperature on Earth is rising.

It is getting too hot for some pollinators. They might die out.

When many pollinators die, it can lead to big problems. For example, fewer crops will grow. People may not have enough food.

Plants also take **greenhouse gases** out of the air. These gases cause climate change. But if there

Did You Know?

Three out of four crops depend on pollinators.

 The mission blue butterfly is one of many pollinators at risk of dying out.

are fewer pollinators, fewer plants will grow. Then more greenhouse gases will stay in the air. As a result, climate change will get worse.

Chapter 3

Protecting Pollinators

People are helping pollinators in many ways. One way is by making pollinator gardens. These gardens include plants that pollinators eat. That way, the animals get enough food. Then they stay in the area.

 Many people grow pollinator gardens at their homes.

The pollinators keep pollinating the crops that people eat.

Pollinator gardens offer more than just food. They also give pollinators a place to live. For example, some pollinators live inside the stems of plants. Others make their homes under leaves.

Did You Know?

Sometimes fruit trees do not get enough pollinators. When that happens, the fruit is smaller. It may also have an odd shape.

 People have helped protect many pollinators, including the lesser long-nosed bat.

Governments have also helped. Some US states have passed laws that protect pollinators' habitats.

 The US Fish and Wildlife Service grew back native prairie in North Dakota. It supports pollinators.

That way, their homes will not be cleared away. Other states have laws about pesticides. Farmers cannot use sprays that harm pollinators.

Governments give money to scientists, too. These scientists try to figure out better ways to help pollinators. Governments have also tried to slow climate change. But scientists agree that much more needs to be done.

Did You Know?

Some governments help people learn about pollinators. That way, more people understand why pollinators matter. And they will be more likely to help.

School Gardens

Many schools grow pollinator gardens. In one school, students caught insects in the school's garden. They counted pollinators to find out which ones were the most common.

In 2020, a **virus** spread around the world. Being inside with many people was unsafe. So, students could not go to school. But they could still help pollinators. One class grew flowers at their homes. Later, the students planted their flowers in the school's pollinator garden. Another class made gardens at home. Each student got a packet of seeds. They grew flowers for bees. Even a small garden can be helpful.

Students plant a pollinator garden in New York.

Chapter 4

How to Help

You can do many things to help pollinators. Planting a garden is one idea. Use plants that are native to your area. Use several kinds of plants. They should **bloom** at different times of year.

 A hummingbird feeds from the flower of a bleeding heart plant.

That way, the pollinators will always have food to eat. Try not to use pesticides. You can avoid harming the pollinators.

Different pollinators eat different things. So, find out which plants will attract certain ones. For example, monarch butterflies seek out milkweed. Hummingbirds often visit flowers that are red. Bees go to many different kinds of plants. Sunflowers and mint are two examples.

> **Monarch caterpillars eat only the leaves of milkweed.**

When more people plant gardens, pollinators will have more places to eat. So, talk to your neighbors. Talk to your teachers, too. You can start a pollinator garden at your school.

Or you can start a garden in your neighborhood.

Lawmakers have the power to make even bigger changes. Let them know that you care about pollinators. Ask them to make stronger rules for pesticides. Also, ask them to set aside large pieces

Did You Know?

Pollinators need water. You can fill a bowl and put it in a garden. Or you can create a small puddle of mud.

 Lawmakers can protect existing pollinator habitats. They can also help grow new habitats.

of land for pollinators. Grasslands

are very important. By working

together, we can help pollinators

stay healthy and safe.

FOCUS ON
Pollinator Gardens

Write your answers on a separate piece of paper.

1. Write a paragraph that explains the main ideas of Chapter 2.

2. Where would you build a pollinator garden in your community? Why?

3. What can harm pollinators?
   A. pesticides
   B. milkweed
   C. grasslands

4. Why is it important to contact lawmakers?
   A. They are better at finding plants that pollinators eat.
   B. They can make bigger changes to help pollinators.
   C. They know the best places to create gardens.

5. What does **threats** mean in this book?

*However, pollinators are facing **threats**. One problem is habitat loss.*

    A. things that pollinators eat

    B. things that will go away quickly

    C. things that can cause harm

6. What does **attract** mean in this book?

*So, find out which plants will **attract** certain ones. For example, monarch butterflies seek out milkweed.*

    A. to make something come closer

    B. to move farther away from something

    C. to keep something where it is

Answer key on page 32.

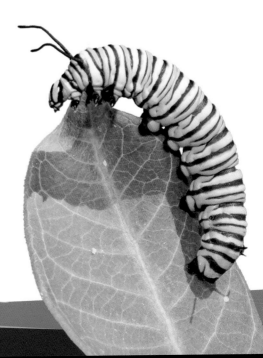

Glossary

bloom
To produce flowers.

climate change
A human-caused global crisis involving long-term changes in Earth's temperature and weather patterns.

greenhouse gases
Gases in the air that trap heat from the sun.

habitat
The type of place where plants or animals normally grow or live.

native
Living or growing naturally in a particular region.

pesticides
Chemicals that kill unwanted plants or animals.

virus
A tiny substance that can cause illness in people and animals.

To Learn More

BOOKS

Brown, Renata Fossen. *Green Gardening: Fun Experiments to Learn, Grow, Harvest, Make, and Play*. Minneapolis: Quarto Publishing Group, 2018.

Bullard, Lisa. *We Need Bees*. Lake Elmo, MN: Focus Readers, 2019.

London, Martha. *Pollinators: Animals Helping Plants Thrive*. Minneapolis: Abdo Publishing, 2020.

NOTE TO EDUCATORS

Visit **www.focusreaders.com** to find lesson plans, activities, links, and other resources related to this title.

Index

B
bats, 10
bees, 5, 10, 20, 24
beetles, 10
butterflies, 5, 10, 24

F
flowers, 5–6, 9, 20, 24

H
habitats, 10, 17
hummingbirds, 6, 24

I
insects, 6, 10, 20

N
nectar, 5–6

P
pesticides, 10, 18, 24, 26
pollen, 9

S
schools, 20, 25
scientists, 19

Answer Key: 1. Answers will vary; **2.** Answers will vary; **3.** A; **4.** B; **5.** C; **6.** A